Voluntude

An Offering

AE Reiff

Grand Canal Flyway
2023

For Teddy

Acknowledgments to *Isreads* that once
posted "Talk" in public places with maps
to their locations in Champaign-Urbana,
on the North LaSalle St. bridge in Chicago,
in Stillwater, OK and elsewhere, now on
Flickr, others at *Frigg, Uppagus, Roadside
Raven Review, Ink Pantry, Plum Tree
Tavern, Kitchen Sink Magazine, Silver
Pinion, Penny Poetry Blog* and
Nomaterialism Journal V to whose editors
gratefully acknowledgement is made.

CONTENTS

Walk in Kilns

One cry up it sounds like light,
Octaves, notes and voice,
that shine in halls where fingers walk
like hymnist's feet on moss.

Voices are heard through walls.
The plain debris of past on rock
of cries and groans takes off,
A crusty top to bypass thought
breaks light for what is hoped.

Off with the hat, hair, eyes, skin, teeth,
Sail woods you think you know,
be snow-cold air at home in years,
take life among the clouds.
Lay hands upon the incandescent tinge
To kindle light, that's how to walk in
kilns.

Holy Ghost Cement

Hopkins left the world unchanged.
Who else need try the ooze of oil,
shook foil, Holy Ghost brood?
We favor Herbert's command.
God's Grandeur lives or dies.
What falls between is vain.
Words to defend against bandits
vibrate around those we love.
How else guard?

Yesterday angels came to a house
that armed robbers feared,
"He guards the lives of his faithful ones,"
"Holy Father, protect them by the power
of your Name, the Name you gave me."
Up on a ladder with scaffold and boards,
with faith I am building the Name with
the Word.

Candles

Breath wears clothes where faces shine
As dream clothes ache for light,
To give heart-people illumined shrines
That alabaster breaks.

A mother brings her offspring into town,
folded arm in arm,
She wears a serape dress of years
To walk among the crowds.

I hollow out a crawlspace in the attic floor
to keep this resolution strong,
to bear in mind the refuge and the breath,
word of mouth to those who flee the wars.

Breath

When it comes to talk
everything is song,
a water breath for gills
breathes song and sings,
breathe song and sing,
they sing, they sing,
Everything has breath.
Everything that has breath.

Everything with breath connects
beneath the silent disconnect,
pure as flame that disappears
in sight and sound forget.

It comes to all who breathe
that water breath, gill song,
a temporary exhalation
that everything else that will have breath
is breathing all along.

Yourself, to meditate a roof below,
communes a creature like no other,
so unique at times at least to say
no matter what I knew that day
when everything had breath. Here I am.

Breath inspires talk,
language, expression, thought,
suddenness of wings,
a base of wind, of dust and sun,
cry of a moment, each moment timed,
three hundred eternal
breathes with the same.
Anything that's done or so recalls
is breathing the same breath as all.

That's what breath in search of talk
like any unique thing means,
Sound of breath.
Everything seeks song unconfined,
for air and water breathers' breath of gills
breathe life, breathe song and sing.
They sing.
They sing.
Everything has breath.
Everything has breath.
Everything that has breath.

When the Cogwheels Came

When the cogwheels came
I was driving late,
etheric wheels in the sky,
a wheel in the middle of a wheel,
two hands held gold flares.

Reasons I made up for this:
the oven not completely baked,
I am cold but it's hot,
the future is not known,
I saw those things without knowing.

Close the curtain, turn out the light,
Bolivian wool over shoulders
lies in a fragile age of sleep.
Guardians watch my driving
like I am a blowing leaf,
or seeing in the faces sky.

Transparencies for rooting need a priest
for lily skin, the joints to home.
Avenues of this city can't be touched,
to speak of a place the water fed,
streams before the river wet,
fed currents, boats and flood.

I pace the lines, fathom the bends,
oxygen leaving lungs.
Libérer le symbole played in my head
in a ditty of water by swans,
the literal rose and rising sun,
sheered down to light before tongue.

Those who died among the flowers
remember in the blood,
brain making sense, replicated order,
the mind's body in the heart,
cogwheel visions of light to consecrate
the service to start.

East River Drive

There, three hours after 11:22, now
2 hours 58 minutes, I will be born.
My father rolls West River Drive
Singing at the top of his lungs.
This must be what he sang, "to your right
See all things done in the body,
in the center is the spiritual destroyed
and on your left forgiveness for sins
so great that it covers the world.

I Poured Out My Tongue

I poured out my tongue,
undid the cork,
my lungs blew breath,
words formed a froth,
bouqueted a cup,
like oil dripped
in what I meant,
I drank them up,
I gave my cheeks to them.

That did inspire wine,
a prayer was sung.
Give your breath
I pray my son
In all books end to end.
To forgive and be forgiven
is the yeast the words give up.
Give me to sup and pour out peace
World without end without end.

Thank Ship

Move up the gang plank,
thanks for the salt,
Thanks for the butter,
for healing the dog,
for helping the cops,
for healing the child,
for protecting neighbors,
for healing awhile.

For love, for Dad,
for peace, for Mom
Thanks for the dolphin,
the grass at our feet,
Thanks for the waters
that live in the sea,
Earth each great species,
each species each,

Thanks to soothe waters,
anoint, bless.
Thanks that I may
breathe this breath.
Thanks I may
lay down and rest,
Blessing, salvation and trees.

Back Pew

Everything I tell you now is true,
I sit in the front or back pew,
My feet hurt but it happens as said,
the back of the hair parted
and locks changed color in forgiveness.
Large people with headaches
after a rough week of aspirins
speak like Hopkins,
there will be light, there will be light.

Passion stands up for thanksgiving,
its name notwithstanding well known,
but it's not my name I came to sing.
Trees grow in the window glass,
Collections are quiet, nobody wears a coat,
silence grows too. I get in trouble
sitting at the back among heavy smokers
and their beer carts living happily
after nosebleeds where people hold hands.

Voluntude

In a life of secret prayer the shoulders
Slump and belly prays for blemished skin,
sudden gestures sweep the hands,
the mind thins.
A wife will nudge her husband's
shoulders with her own,
foreheads protected with the rib of palms
plead deliverance for a cradled thumb,
voice patterns sputter, twist to the sun,
pray without ceasing,
that's what they do,
If mind and voice won't pray,
the groans are voluntude.

Fifteen Words

It's easy to pray when I clean the blood,
fifteen words laid on the wound.
It's easier to pray than you think
With the eyes wet.
I pray wisdom with a shovel
To speak those.

Lodger

Lodger goes on hands and feet
except he has a head.
There is a cowl,
but nothing in the shell.
Does that tell you where he's gone?
He knows his life is not his own.

Work ground brother, turn flesh mother,
is your milk in dugs?
Coyote what you cover,
cornstalk, robe what fill?
With no head you stand him up
but he flows through.

The Sound of Light

The sound of light wakes up and down
echoed in silence alone.
Layered as a symphony might,
but sound does not broadcast light
To keep in shouts and groans,
it stands alone.

To figure the days it has been out,
The decade sublunar years I count,
One octave cry, a wave, a chord.
Toes sing, hands dance as might
a hymnist who plays on moss,
eyes shining in halls,
whose fingers are heard through walls.

The World's Body

The spiritual did not come first
but the natural, and after that the spiritual.

I lay in bed trying to get my breath,
slept a long hour or two before dawn,
gradually I became aware my body
had risen slightly from its sleeping form.
This felt good so I didn't move,
went in and out of sleep several times.
I could hear differently then,
wheezing groans, coughs and forced
breaths
and sounds like long sonorous moans.
I was either asleep in this raised state
hearing my own flesh cry out in pain,
or awake hearing the world's sound,
loud early in night which had since
calmed down.
It was like a train or a moan the world
cried out,
a patient deep in pain this resonant thing
with a mellow groan and travail.
I heard it snoring in some detail.

I conclude from this a spiritual world
                                 exists,
that its spiritual body lacks sense
and that something is terribly wrong
if it makes these sounds like an old folks
                                 home.
Back in flesh I didn't hear it again.

An Issue of Blood

They have left Thee naked Lord, O that they had ;
This Garment too I would they had deny'd
Thee with Thy Self they have too richly clad,
Opening the purple wardrobe of Thy side.
O never could be found Garments too good
For Thee to wear, but these, of thine own blood.
Richard Crashaw

The communion cup leaked,
I didn't spill it!
It got on the book at the edge of the pew.
It felt wet through a crack
When they sang a hymn.
When I put it to my lips
None was left.
The crack got wide
Down at my feet.
It pooled in the rug,
on my clothes and my hands.
The tops of Bibles in the pews overflowed.
I couldn't sing. I couldn't see the screen.

It's one thing to die, another to have blood.
Others may bleed, the flood has been
great,
the blood now staining those who remain
I don't wipe off. The drops are everywhere

Smoking

How do you explain to yourself
what you're doing?
I burned trash on top of the rock
and flames jetted up.
I lay in a chair under Chinaberry limbs
and the cry of the world's body
Began to rock the house.
The explanation of a storm
did not seem plausible.
Houses came over the ridge,
Followed by towns.
We pulled long grasses up by the root,
lit them afire to hurl
from trenches, pits dug as traps,
sailed the afternoon.

I was standing by invitation,
a little out of body
when a moonish face asked,
why have you come? Me?
I want to quit smoking. We knelt.
More bizarre habits from this contract.
I quit drinking. What's better than a
Becks, a Beaujolais, a stout?
I stood in the light and walked
Clothed to the end of the world.

First Step

One good thing the body is
when blanket draws to feet.
Swimming on the bright sea crest
a mind shook oil matured with soil
down the seed coat stretched.

No one gets through birth the same
before eternity rise,
when that back leg steps to light,
out from darkness, day, sun, night,
out of darkness vents flame.

Birth

"I can't look," he says,
seed coats spin from form.
A hand reaches out,
retrieves the flame of words
that come from arms.
Spray water, shake,
the shells fall off,
the egg is born.

Lamb Light

I came to the water and thirsted,
sought for this Lamb Light,
that God given Tree of Life,
I bought this water right.

Who has not seen his limbs outstretched,
boughs with his blessing,
beauty and grace bowed down to us,
fragrant pressing.

When I awoke and thirsted
my roots found this stream.
This Christmas as intended
I go in.

Wayfarer

The name of the city, had no light,
exterior immersed in sleep.
Trees on both sides watered fruit,
Each, for the water flowed deep

Waking answers to prayers,
ordered before they were prayed,
we wake to walk from labyrinths
and lightning rods from graves.

Signs and Wonders

A cello in the story of Van Gogh's head
made its music falling down,
that wind blew Hopkins' mansion,
burned in manuscripts behind Blake's
house.
Artists were shaken from their shelf.
There in the basket of this art would lie
the Lamb without a blemish or a spot,
whose fellowship the author got
in signs that gouge a flame of sparks,
a sea of tildas on nimbus heads, to plow
commas and question marks before men
awake from sleep remove their shrouds.

www.ingramcontent.com/pod-product-compliance
Lightning Source LLC
Chambersburg PA
CBHW060708280326
41933CB00012B/2349